وَرَتِّلِ الْقُرْآنَ تَرْتِيلًا

A Classical Primer on Tajwīd

Sheikh Sulaymān al-Jamzūrī's

Tuḥfat al-Aṭfāl

with points from Ibn al-Jazarī's

Muqaddimah

دار الثقافة
Dar Ul Thaqafah

Dar Ul Thaqafah

www.darulthaqafah.com
www.facebook.com/darulthaqafah
www.twitter.com/darulthaqafah

2023 CE – 1444 H

Translation of the Qur'ān

It should be perfectly clear that the Qur'ān is only authentic in its original language, Arabic. Since perfect translation of the Qur'ān is impossible, we have used the translation of the meaning of the Qur'ān throughout the book, as the result is only a crude meaning of the Arabic text.

Qur'ānic verses appear in speech marks proceeded by a reference to the Surah and verse number. Sayings (*Hadith*) of Prophet Muhammad ρ appear in inverted commas along with reference to the Hadith Book and its Reporter.

Contents

Translator's Introduction

Tajwīd (tr. 'making something good or better') is the discipline of proper Qur'anic recitation. It involves pronouncing each letter from its proper point of articulation and giving it its due attributes consistently. It is acquired by listening to those who have mastered it, emulating them, and being tested. Learning the theoretical rules of tajwīd is a communal obligation (Ar. *farḍ kifāyah*) while practicing it is an individual obligation (Ar. *farḍ ʿayn*).

What follows is a complete, annotated translation of Sheikh Sulaymān al-Jamzūrī's *Tuḥfat al-Aṭfāl*, a classical didactic poem on tajwīd. The poem covers the bare essentials of tajwīd, including: rules related to the pronunciation of *nūn* and *mīm*, long vowels (Ar. *mudūd*), sun and moon letters, and an introduction to the theoretical basis for the assimilation of various letters. Each group of related verses is first translated in a somewhat literal fashion, followed by an explanation of the rules contained in it, and finally elucidated with examples. Constructs in the original Arabic that are present merely for the sake of versification are not translated, as they would only serve to distract. In addition to this introductory poem, the section on points of articulation (Ar. *maḵārij al-ḥurūf*) from Imam Ibn al-Jazarī's intermediate-level poem on tajwīd is included.

Other than the numbered verses of poetry in either language, everything that appears in the text is the endeavour of the translator. *Caveat lector*.

May Allah accept this work and make it a means to implement the Prophet's words ﷺ, "The best amongst you is the one who learns the Qur'an and teaches it."

Moustafa Elqabbany
October 2016 | Muharram 1438

Transliteration Guide

Whereas a non-technical text may be well-suited to simplified transliteration, a text whose subject matter is precise pronunciation must necessarily employ precise transliteration. Using letter combinations such as *sh* and *kh* to represent single sounds each presents a problem when one actually intends both sounds individually, such as in the Arabic word '*ashal*' (tr. 'easier'). Furthermore, when such consonants are doubled, transliterating them becomes rather sloppy: the Arabic word for brain, for example, would be written as '*mukhkh*', which is difficult to read. Additionally, the letter combination *th* represents two distinct sounds in English, and three in Arabic. Such ambiguity is not acceptable in a text concerned with Qur'anic recitation. For this reason, a single, unique character is used for each Arabic letter.

Standard Arabic vowels are represented by the letters: *a*, *i*, and *u*; long vowels are *ā*, *ī*, and *ū*. The *hamzah* is represented as such: ʾ. By way of example, the word "Qur'an" would be transliterated as *qurʾān*.

The Arabic alphabet is transliterated as below:

alif	ا	ḍād	ض
bāʾ	ب	ṭāʾ	ط
tāʾ	ت	ẓāʾ	ظ
ṯāʾ	ث	ʿayn	ع
jīm	ج	ġayn	غ
ḥāʾ	ح	fāʾ	ف
ḵāʾ	خ	qāf	ق
dāl	د	kāf	ك
ḏāl	ذ	lām	ل
rāʾ	ر	mīm	م
zāy	ز	nūn	ن
sīn	س	hāʾ	ه
šīn	ش	wāw	و
ṣād	ص	yāʾ	ي

Tuḥfat al-Aṭfāl

Sheikh Sulaymān al-Jamzūrī

The Poem's Introduction
(Lines 1–5)

1 يَقُولُ رَاجِي رَحْمَةِ الْغَفُورِ   دَوْمًا سُلَيْمَانُ هُوَ الْجَمْزُورِي

2 الْحَمْدُ لِلَّهِ مُصَلِّيًا عَلَى   مُحَمَّدٍ وَآلِهِ وَمَنْ تَلَا

3 وَبَعْدُ هَذَا النَّظْمُ لِلْمُرِيدِ   فِي النُّونِ وَالتَّنْوِينِ وَالْمُدُودِ

4 سَمَّيْتُهُ بِتُحْفَةِ الأَطْفَالِ   عَنْ شَيْخِنَا الْمِيهِيِّ ذِي الْكَمَالِ

5 أَرْجُو بِهِ أَنْ يَنْفَعَ الطُّلَّابَا   وَالأَجْرَ وَالْقَبُولَ وَالثَّوَابَا

1 *Sulaymān al-Jamzūri, who constantly seeks the Mercy of the Oft-Forgiving, says:*

2 *Praise be to Allah, while sending blessings upon Muhammad, his people, and those who follow [him].*

3 *Now then, this poem is for students on the subject of nūn, tanwīn, and long vowels.*

4 *I have named it 'The Children's Gift' on behalf of our perfected sheikh, al-Mīhī.*

5 *I hope that it benefits students, and [hope for] a reward, acceptance, and a goodly requital.*

The Four Cases of the Vowelless *Nūn* and *Tanwīn*
(Line 6)

6 لِلنُّونِ إِنْ تَسْكُنْ وَلِلتَّنْوِينِ   أَرْبَعُ أَحْكَامٍ فَخُذْ تَبْيِينِي

6 *The vowelless nūn and tanwīn have four cases, so receive my explanation.*

Tanwīn is pronounced identically to a vowelless *nūn*, which is why the two are treated together. The main difference between them is that, whereas a vowelless *nūn* can occur anywhere in a word (other than as the first letter), *tanwīn* only occurs at the end of a word.

There are four cases that govern the proper pronunciation of the vowelless *nūn* and *tanwīn* that the author will elucidate shortly. What distinguishes one case from another is the letter that follows the vowelless *nūn* or *tanwīn*. This phenomenon is true whether the following letter is in a different word (which it must be in the case of *tanwīn*) or the same word.

Case 1 of the Vowelless *Nūn* and *Tanwīn*: Enunciation
(Lines 7–8)

7 فَالأَوَّلُ الإِظْهَارُ قَبْلَ أَحْرُفِ   لِلْحَلْقِ سِتٍّ رُتِّبَتْ فَلْتَعْرِفِ

8 هَمْزٌ فَهَاءٌ ثُمَّ عَيْنٌ حَاءُ   مُهْمَلَتَانِ ثُمَّ غَيْنٌ خَاءُ

7 *The first [case] is enunciation [when the nūn or tanwīn comes] before six guttural letters, in order:*

8 *Hamzah and hā', then 'ayn and ḥā', undotted, then ġayn and ḵā'.*

If a vowelless *nūn* or *tanwīn* immediately precedes one of the six letters mentioned in line 8, it falls under the case of enunciation (Ar. *iẓhār*), meaning that the *n* sound is pronounced clearly, without modifying its sound in the slightest. It is also not pronounced with extended nasalization (Ar. *ġunnah*), other than what is necessary to pronounce the *n* sound naturally.

These six letters all arise from the throat (Ar. *ḥalq*), which is what is meant by 'guttural' in this context, even though this term is not linguistically precise. The author lists the letters in the order of their place of articulation (Ar. *maḵraj*): *hamzah* and *hā'* are the furthest back; *'ayn* and *ḥā'* are further forward; finally, *ġayn* and *ḵā'* occur at the front of the throat.

The author's mention of the letters as being 'undotted' is not merely filler: defective Arabic printings sometimes miss dots, and splattered ink sometimes gives the reader the impression that dots exists where they do not. Thus, explicitly mentioning which letters are dotted clarifies the author's intent.

Examples of enunciation are detailed in the chart below:

Letter	Medial Vowelless *Nūn*	Final Vowelless *Nūn*	*Tanwīn*
hamzah	﴿وَيَنْـَٔوْنَ﴾ *(Al-Anʿām,* 6:26*)*	﴿مَنْ ءَامَنَ﴾ *(Al-Baqarah,* 2:62*)*	﴿وَجَنَّٰتٍ أَلْفَافًا﴾ *(An-Nabaʾ,* 78:16*)*
hāʾ	﴿مِنْهَا﴾ *(Al-Baqarah,* 2:25*)*	﴿مَنْ هَاجَرَ﴾ *(Al-Ḥašr,* 59:9*)*	﴿جُرُفٍ هَارٍ﴾ *(At-Tawbah,* 9:109*)*
ʿayn	﴿أَنْعَمْتَ﴾ *(Al-Fātiḥah,* 1:7*)*	﴿مِنْ عِلْمٍ﴾ *(An-Nisāʾ,* 4:157*)*	﴿حَقِيقٌ عَلَىٰٓ﴾ *(Al-Aʿrāf,* 7:105*)*
ḥāʾ	﴿يَنْحِتُونَ﴾ *(Al-Ḥijr,* 15:82*)*	﴿مَنْ حَآدَّ﴾ *(Al-Mujādilah,* 58:22*)*	﴿عَلِيمٌ حَكِيمٌ﴾ *(An-Nisāʾ,* 4:26*)*
ġayn	﴿فَسَيُنْغِضُونَ﴾ *(Al-Isrāʾ,* 17:51*)*	﴿مِّنْ غِلٍّ﴾ *(Al-Aʿrāf,* 7:43*)*	﴿حَلِيمًا غَفُورًا﴾ *(Al-Isrāʾ,* 17:44*)*
ḵāʾ	﴿وَٱلْمُنْخَنِقَةُ﴾ *(Al-Māʾidah,* 5:3*)*	﴿لِمَنْ خَافَ﴾ *(Hūd,* 11:103*)*	﴿يَوْمَئِذٍ خَٰشِعَةٌ﴾ *(Al-Ġāšiyah,* 88:2*)*

Case 2 of the Vowelless *Nūn* and *Tanwīn*: Assimilation
(Lines 9–12)

9 وَالثَّانِ إِدْغَامٌ بِسِتَّةٍ أَتَتْ   فِي يَرْمُلُونَ عِنْدَهُمْ قَدْ ثَبَتَتْ

10 لَكِنَّهَا قِسْمَانِ قِسْمٌ يُدْغَمَا   فِيْهِ بِغُنَّةٍ بِيَنْمُو عُلِمَا

11 إِلَّا إِذَا كَانَا بِكِلْمَةٍ فَلا   تُدْغِمْ كَدُنْيَا ثُمَّ صِنْوَانٍ تَلا

12 وَالثَّانِ إِدْغَامٌ بِغَيْرِ غُنَّهْ   فِي اللَّامِ وَالرَّا ثُمَّ كَرِّرَنَّهْ

9 *The second [case] is assimilation with six [letters] whose established mnemonic is 'yarmulūn'.*[1]

10 *However, it is of two types: assimilation with nasalization—which is known by [the letters] 'yanmū'.*

11 *But if both [the nūn followed by the given letter] are in a single word, do not assimilate, such as [in the words] 'dunyā' and 'ṣinwān'.*

12 *Secondly is assimilation without nasalization with [the letters] lām and rā', and make sure to repeat it [(i.e. the rā')].*

If a vowelless *nūn* or *tanwīn* immediately precedes one of six letters present in the mnemonic '*yarmulūn*' (tr. 'they trot') —i.e. the *yā'*, *rā'*, *mīm*, *lām*, *wāw*, or *nūn*—it falls under the case of assimilation

1 A common mispronunciation is *yarmalūn*. The vowel following the *mīm* is *u*, not *a*.

(Ar. *idġām*), meaning that the *n* sound is merged into the letter after it.

Assimilation is of two types: nasalized and non-nasalized. Nasalized assimilation occurs with four of the six letters mentioned earlier: the *yāʾ*, *nūn*, *mīm* and *wāw*, whose combined mnemonic is '*yanmū*' (tr. 'it grows'). The *n* sound that precedes these four letters disappears such that the letter following it is doubled, but with extended nasalization. So, in addition to doubling the letter that the *n* sound is assimilated into, the reciter actually extends the doubled letter's pronunciation further to emphasize the nasalization.

Non-nasalized assimilation occurs with the two remaining letters: *lām* and *rāʾ*. The *n* sound disappears entirely and the letter following it is doubled naturally. Unlike the previous case of nasalized assimilation, the doubled letter's pronunciation is not extended beyond what is called for in normal Arabic speech.

Assimilation of both types occurs only between words, and never in a single word. In verse 11, the author explicitly negates intra-word nasalized assimilation. (He does not explicitly negate intra-word non-nasalized assimilation, possibly because there is no need to: nowhere in the Qur'an is there a medial vowelless nūn followed by a *lām* or *rāʾ*.) There are four words in the Qur'an which a beginner might be tempted to recite with assimilation. However, because they are intra-word occurrences, one enunciates instead of assimilating. The words are: *ṣinwān* (*Ar-Raʿd*, 13:4), *qinwān* (*Al-Anʿām*, 6:99), *bunyān* (*Aṣ-Ṣaff*, 61:4), and *dunyā* (which occurs 111 times in the Qur'an).

Examples of nasalized assimilation are detailed in the chart below:

Letter	Final Vowelless *Nūn*	*Tanwīn*
yā'	﴿مَن يَقُولُ﴾ (*Al-Baqarah*, 2:8)	﴿وَبَرْقٌ يَجْعَلُونَ﴾ (*Al-Baqarah*, 2:19)
nūn	﴿مِن نُّورٍ﴾ (*An-Nūr*, 24:40)	﴿يَوْمَئِذٍ نَّاعِمَةٌ﴾ (*Al-Ġāšiyah*, 88:8)
mīm	﴿مِمَّن مَّنَعَ﴾ (*Al-Baqarah*, 2:114)	﴿مَثَلًا مَّا﴾ (*Al-Baqarah*, 2:26)
wāw	﴿مِن وَالٍ﴾ (*Ar-Ra'd*, 13:11)	﴿غِشَاوَةٌ وَلَهُمْ﴾ (*Al-Baqarah*, 2:7)

Examples of non-nasalized assimilation are detailed in the chart below:

Letter	Final Vowelless *Nūn*	*Tanwīn*
lām	﴿وَلَٰكِن لَّا يَعْلَمُونَ﴾ (*Al-Baqarah*, 2:13)	﴿هُدًى لِّلْمُتَّقِينَ﴾ (*Al-Baqarah*, 2:2)
rā'	﴿مِّن رَّبِّهِمْ﴾ (*Al-Baqarah*, 2:5)	﴿ثَمَرَةٍ رِّزْقًا﴾ (*Al-Baqarah*, 2:25)

At the end of line 12, the author points out an attribute specific to the letter *rā'*: repetition. Scholars of tajwīd differ in how they treat this attribute, with some saying that it must be avoided entirely and others, such as the author of this text, affirming its importance. What is established beyond a doubt by all scholars and masters of tajwīd is that rolling the *rāʾ* (like in the Spanish word *perro*) is forbidden while reciting the Qur'an. Those who maintain that repetition of the *rāʾ* is necessary intend by it a very subtle vibration of the tip of the tongue that results from air being forced through the small passage between the tongue's tip and the palate.

Case 3 of the Vowelless *Nūn* and *Tanwīn*: Transformation
(Line 13)

13 وَالثَّالِثُ الإِقْلَابُ عِنْدَ الْبَاءِ   مِيمًا بِغُنَّةٍ مَعَ الإِخْفَاءِ

13 The third [case] is transformation into a mīm with nasalization and weakening at [the letter] bāʾ.

If a vowelless *nūn*—whether medial or final—or *tanwīn* immediately precedes the letter *bāʾ*, it is replaced with a *mīm*[2] with extended nasalization, meaning the reciter lengthens the pronunciation of the *mīm* beyond its usual duration. The usual Arabic pronunciation of *mīm* involves pressing the lips together firmly, more than is usual for native speakers of English. However, when a *nūn* or *tanwīn* is transformed into a *mīm*, the lips are not pressed

2 This is similar to the English transformation of 'grandpa' into 'grampa'.

together as firmly as normal, and this is what the author intends by 'weakening' (Ar. *ikfā'*).

Examples of transformation (Ar. *iqlāb*) are detailed in the chart below:

Letter	Medial Vowelless *Nūn*	Final Vowelless *Nūn*	*Tanwīn*
bā'	﴿أَنۢبِئۡهُم﴾ *(Al-Baqarah, 2:33)*	﴿أَنۢ بُورِكَ﴾ *(An-Naml, 27:8)*	﴿سَمِيعُۢ بَصِيرٌ﴾ *(Al-Ḥajj, 22:61)*

Case 4 of the Vowelless *Nūn* and *Tanwīn*: Weak Pronunciation
(Lines 14–16)

14 وَالرَّابِعُ الإِخْفَاءُ عِنْدَ الْفَاضِلِ مِنَ الْحُرُوفِ وَاجِبٌ لِلْفَاضِلِ

15 فِي خَمْسَةٍ مِنْ بَعْدِ عَشْرٍ رَمْزُهَا فِي كِلْمِ هَذَا الْبَيْتِ قَدْ ضَمَّنْتُهَا

16 صِفْ ذَا ثَنَا كَمْ جَادَ شَخْصٌ قَدْ سَمَا دُمْ طَيِّبًا زِدْ فِي تُقًى ضَعْ ظَالِمَا

14 *The fourth [case] is weak pronunciation with the remaining letters, being obligatory upon the meritorious.*

15 *With fifteen letters whose mnemonic I have included in the words of this verse:*

16 *'Describe a praiseworthy person. How great is one ennobled! Stay well. Increase in piety. Put down an oppressor.'*

Verse 16 consists of fifteen Arabic words. The first letter of each word is unique and significant. If a vowelless *nūn* (whether medial or final) or *tanwīn* immediately precedes any one of these fifteen letters, it is pronounced weakly[3] by preparing oneself to pronounce the letter after the *nūn* or *tanwīn* and then nasalizing for an extended duration while one's mouth is in that position. Because the points of articulation of the various letters differ greatly, nasalization will sound different for the various letters. There are seven emphatic letters in Arabic: *ḵā*ʾ, *ṣād, ḍād, ṭā*ʾ, *ẓā*ʾ, *ġayn,* and *qāf.* Five of these—all but *ḵā*ʾ and *ġayn*—are also from among the fifteen letters mentioned in this section. When nasalization is effected before these letters, it will naturally sound emphatic because one has already prepared the point of articulation for the letter after the *nūn* or *tanwīn,* which is in itself emphatic.

Examples of weak pronunciation (Ar. *iḵfā*ʾ) are detailed in the chart below:

Letter	**Medial Vowelless *Nūn***	**Final Vowelless *Nūn***	***Tanwīn***
ṣād	﴿وَيَنصُرْكُمْ﴾ *(At-Tawbah,* 9:14*)*	﴿أَن صَدُّوكُمْ﴾ *(Al-Mā'idah,* 5:2*)*	﴿رِيحًا صَرْصَرًا﴾ *(Fuṣṣilat,* 41:16*)*
ḏāl	﴿مُنذِرٌ﴾ *(Ar-Ra'd,* 13:7*)*	﴿مِّن ذَكَرٍ﴾ *(Āl-'Imrān,* 3:195*)*	﴿سِرَاعًا ذَٰلِكَ﴾ *(Qāf,* 50:44*)*

3 An example of this in English is how the letter n is pronounced in the word 'ink'.

Letter	Medial Vowelless *Nūn*	Final Vowelless *Nūn*	*Tanwīn*
ṯā'	﴿مَّنثُورًا﴾ *(Al-Furqān,* 25:23*)*	﴿مِن ثَمَرَةٍ﴾ *(Al-Baqarah,* 2:25*)*	﴿جَمِيعًا ثُمَّ﴾ *(Al-Baqarah,* 2:29*)*
kāf	﴿يَنكُثُونَ﴾ *(Al-A'rāf,* 7:135*)*	﴿مَن كَانَ﴾ *(Al-Baqarah,* 2:97*)*	﴿عَادًا كَفَرُوا۟﴾ *(Hūd,* 11:60*)*
jīm	﴿فَأَنجَيْنَـٰهُ﴾ *(Al- A'rāf,* 7:64*)*	﴿أَن جَآءَكُمْ﴾ *(Al-A'rāf,* 7:63*)*	﴿شَيْـًٔا جَنَّـٰتِ﴾ *(Maryam,* 19:60-61*)*
šīn	﴿يُنشِئُ﴾ *(Al-'Ankabūt,* 29:20*)*	﴿مَن شَآءَ﴾ *(Al-Furqān,* 25:57*)*	﴿عَلِيمٌ شَرَعَ﴾ *(Aš-Šūrā,* 42:12-13*)*
qāf	﴿مُنقَلِبُونَ﴾ *(Al-A'rāf,* 7:125*)*	﴿وَلَئِن قُتِلْتُمْ﴾ *(Āl-'Imrān,* 3:157*)*	﴿شَىْءٍ قَدِيرٌ﴾ *(Al-Baqarah,* 2:20*)*
sīn	﴿مِنسَأَتَهُۥ﴾ *(Saba',* 34:14*)*	﴿مِن سُوٓءٍ﴾ *(Āl-'Imrān,* 3:30*)*	﴿عَـٰبِدَٰتٍ سَـٰٓئِحَـٰتٍ﴾ *(At-Taḥrīm,* 66:5*)*
dāl	﴿أَندَادًا﴾ *(Al-Baqarah,* 2:22*)*	﴿مِن دَآبَّةٍ﴾ *(Al- An'ām,* 6:38*)*	﴿قِنْوَانٌ دَانِيَةٌ﴾ *(Al- An'ām,* 6:99*)*
ṭā'	﴿يَنطِقُونَ﴾ *(Al-Anbiyā',* 21:63*)*	﴿مِن طَيِّبَـٰتِ﴾ *(Al-Baqarah,* 2:57*)*	﴿حَلَـٰلًا طَيِّبًا﴾ *(Al-Baqarah,* 2:168*)*
zāy	﴿يُنزَفُونَ﴾ *(Aṣ-Ṣāffāt,* 37:47*)*	﴿فَإِن زَلَلْتُم﴾ *(Al-Baqarah,* 2:209*)*	﴿يَوْمَئِذٍ زُرْقًا﴾ *(Ṭā-Hā,* 20:102*)*
fā'	﴿ٱلْأَنفَالِ﴾ *(Al-Anfāl,* 8:1*)*	﴿وَإِن فَاتَكُمْ﴾ *(Al-Mumtaḥanah,* 60:11*)*	﴿سَوْءٍ فَـٰسِقِينَ﴾ *(Al-Anbiyā',* 21:74*)*

Letter	Medial Vowelless *Nūn*	Final Vowelless *Nūn*	*Tanwīn*
tā'	﴿أَنتَ﴾ *(Al-Baqarah,* 2:32*)*	﴿فَمَن تَابَ﴾ *(Al-Mā'idah,* 5:39*)*	﴿جَنَّٰتٍ تَجۡرِى﴾ *(Al-Baqarah,* 2:25*)*
ḍād	﴿مَّنضُودٖ﴾ *(Hūd,* 11:82*)*	﴿مَّن ضَلَّ﴾ *(Al-Mā'idah,* 5:105*)*	﴿مَسۡجِدٗا ضِرَارٗا﴾ *(At-Tawbah,* 9:107*)*
ẓā'	﴿تَنظُرُونَ﴾ *(Al-Baqarah,* 2:50*)*	﴿مَن ظُلِمَ﴾ *(An-Nisā',* 4:148*)*	﴿قَوۡمٖ ظَلَمُوٓاْ﴾ *(Āl-'Imrān,* 3:117*)*

The Doubled *Mīm* and *Nūn*
(Line 17)

17 وَغُنَّ مِيمًا ثُمَّ نُونًا شُدِّدَا   وَسَمِّ كُلًّا حَرْفَ غُنَّةٍ بَدَا

17 Nasalize mīm and nūn when doubled and name each a 'nasalized letter'.

Nasalization is an intrinsic attribute of both the *mīm* and *nūn*, meaning that the letters cannot be pronounced properly without it. This is true even if they are pronounced weakly. However, when they are doubled, they must be clearly enunciated, and the pronunciation is extended longer than is necessary for normal Arabic speech. As mentioned earlier, when pronouncing the *mīm*, the lips are pressed together more than they are when pronouncing the English letter *m*. Extended nasalization is effected whether the doubled *mīm* or *nūn* is in its medial or final position.

Examples of the doubled *mīm* and *nūn* are detailed in the chart below:

Doubled Letter	Medial Position	Final Position
mīm	﴿لَمَّا﴾ *(Al-An'ām, 6:5)*	﴿لَهُم مَّن﴾ *(Yūnus, 10:27)*
nūn	﴿مِنَ ٱلْجِنَّةِ﴾ *(An-Nās, 114:6)*	﴿مِّن نَّذِيرٍ﴾ *(Al-Qaṣaṣ, 28:46)*

The Three Cases of the Vowelless *Mīm*

(Lines 18–19)

18 وَالْمِيمُ إِنْ تَسْكُنْ تَجِي قَبْلَ الْهِجَا لا أَلِفٍ لَيِّنَةٍ لِذِي الْحِجَا

19 أَحْكَامُهَا ثَلَاثَةٌ لِمَنْ ضَبَطْ إِخْفَاءٌ ادْغَامٌ وَإِظْهَارٌ فَقَطْ

18 *When unvowelled, mīm appears before any letter, other than an alif, [which is clear] to those of sound mind.*

19 *Its cases are three for an exacting person: weak pronunciation, assimilation, and enunciation only.*

An unvowelled *mīm* can appear before any letter other than an *alif*, because the latter is always unvowelled in Arabic and requires the letter before it to carry a *fatḥah*. (Note: the *alif* should not be confused with a *hamzah*, which is often seated on an *alif*.) All other letters, including the *wāw* and *yā'*, can appear after *mīm* if they are themselves vowelled.

Depending on the letter that follows the unvowelled *mīm*, it is pronounced in one of three ways: weakly, assimilated into the letter after it, or enunciated clearly.

Case 1 of the Vowelless *Mīm*: Weak Pronunciation
(Line 20)

20 فَالأَوَّلُ الإِخْفَاءُ عِنْدَ الْبَاءِ وَسَمِّهِ الشَّفْوِيَّ لِلْقُرَّاءِ

20 The first [case] is weak pronunciation before bā' for reciters, and name it 'labial'.

Whenever an unvowelled *mīm* appears before a *bā'*, it is pronounced weakly, meaning that the lips are not pressed together as firmly as they are when pronouncing the *mīm* normally (which is stronger in Arabic than in English).[4] The nasalized

4 It is important to note that the lips must still be pressed together during weak pronunciation, albeit less so than when pronouncing *mīm* normally. As for the notion that one must leave a (small) gap between one's lips during labial weakness, it originated in the late 1960s CE. The overseer of *Radio Qur'an* in Cairo at the time was by all measures a great reciter and scholar of tajwīd. However, he reasoned that, just as weak pronunciation of the *nūn* entailed not hitting the exact point of its articulation with the tongue, the reciter must also be required to avoid hitting the exact point of articulation of the *mīm* during its weak pronunciation by leaving a small gap between the lips. The problem with this hypothesis is that it

sound is extended for a duration longer than what is normally needed for the pronunciation of an unvowelled *mīm*. This type of weak pronunciation is called 'labial weakness' (Ar. *iḵfā' šafawī*) because the point of articulation of the *mīm* is the lips. It only occurs when an unvowelled *mīm* is the last letter of a word and a *bā'* is the first letter of the following word. There is no case of an unvowelled *mīm* followed by a *bā'* in the same word in the Qur'an. An example (from *Al-Fīl*, 105:4) is:

﴿تَرْمِيهِم بِحِجَارَةٍ﴾

Case 2 of the Vowelless *Mīm*: Assimilation
(Line 21)

21 وَالثَّانِ إِدْغَامٌ بِمِثْلِهَا أَتَى   وَسَمِّ إِدْغَامًا صَغِيرًا يَا فَتَى

21 The second [case] is assimilation into the same letter, and name it 'minor assimilation', young man.

Whenever an unvowelled *mīm* is followed by another *mīm*, the first is assimilated into the second, which is thereby doubled, and the nasalization is

is not borne out by any of the numerous chains of oral transmission of Qur'anic recitation from teacher to student; i.e. it is an innovation. In addition to teaching this heretofore unknown position to his numerous students, the promoter of this idea imposed his opinion on all those who recited for *Radio Qur'an*, which had somewhat of an official standing in the Arab world. The new idea spread throughout Egypt and much of the Arab world.

pronounced for an extended duration. This is a case of minor assimilation, and only occurs when the unvowelled *mīm* is the last letter of a word. (Minor and major assimilation are discussed in detail in a later section.) An example (from *Al-Baqarah*, 2:134) is:

﴿وَلَكُم مَّا كَسَبْتُمْ﴾

Case 3 of the Vowelless *Mīm*: Enunciation
(Line 22)

22 وَالثَّالِثُ الإِظْهَارُ فِي الْبَقِيَّةْ مِنْ أَحْرُفٍ وَسَمِّهَا شَفْوِيَّةْ

22 *The third [case] is enunciation with all remaining letters, and name it 'labial'.*

Whenever an unvowelled *mīm* is followed by any of the remaining 26 Arabic letters (including *hamzah* but not the *alif*, *bā'*, or *mīm*), it is enunciated clearly and completely with nasalization (which is intrinsic to it) but without extending its duration. The lips are pressed together firmly, more so than in English. This holds whether the unvowelled *mīm* is in the medial or final position. This type of enunciation is termed 'labial' because the place of articulation of the *mīm* is the lips.

A Warning Regarding the Unvowelled *Mīm* Before *Wāw* and *Fā'*
(Line 23)

23 وَاحْذَرْ لَدَى وَاوٍ وَفَا أَنْ تَخْتَفِي   لِقُرْبِهَا وَالاتِّحَادِ فَاعْرِفِ

23 *Be careful that it [i.e. mīm] not become weak before wāw or fā' due to the proximity or unity [of point of articulation], so know this!*

Pronouncing the unvowelled *mīm* weakly when it precedes a *wāw* or *fā'* is a common mistake. This should be a case of enunciation, not weak pronunciation. The nasalization of the *mīm* should not be extended and the lips should be pressed firmly together. The reason for this mistake is that the point of articulation of the *mīm* is the same as that of the *wāw* and close to that of the *fā'*.

Examples where enunciation is required are below:

	wāw	*fā'*
mīm	﴿عَلَيْهِمْ وَلَا﴾ *(Al-Fātiḥah, 1:7)*	﴿وَهُمْ فِيهَا﴾ *(Al-Baqarah, 2:25)*

The Two Cases of the *Lām* of *Al-*: Enunciation and Assimilation

(Lines 24–28)

24 لِلَامِ أَلْ حَالَانِ قَبْلَ الأَحْرُفِ   أُولَاهُمَا إِظْهَارُهَا فَلْتَعْرِفِ

25 قَبْلَ ارْبَعٍ مَعْ عَشْرَةٍ خُذْ عِلْمَهُ   مِنِ ابْغِ حَجَّكَ وَخَفْ عَقِيمَهُ

26 ثَانِيهِمَا إِدْغَامُهَا فِي أَرْبَعِ   وَعَشْرَةٍ أَيْضًا وَرَمْزَهَا فَعِ

27 طِبْ ثُمَّ صِلْ رَحْمًا تَفُزْ ضِفْ ذَا نِعَمْ   دَعْ سُوءَ ظَنٍّ زُرْ شَرِيفًا لِلْكَرَمْ

28 وَاللَّامُ الاولَى سَمِّهَا قَمْرِيَّةْ   وَاللَّامُ الاخْرَى سَمِّهَا شَمْسِيَّةْ

24 *The lām of al- has two cases before letters. The first is its enunciation, so know this!*

25 *[It occurs] before fourteen letters, so take its knowledge from, 'Wish for your pilgrimage and fear its futility.'*

26 *The second [case] is its assimilation also into fourteen letters, and note its mnemonic:*

27 *'Be good, then maintain familial relations and you will succeed; be a guest of the well-to-do; abandon ill opinions; visit a nobleman for honour.'*

28 *Name the first lām 'moon-like' and name the other lām 'sun-like'.*

The *lām* of the definite article *al-* has two cases: enunciation and assimilation. The second hemistich of line 25 contains a mnemonic Arabic sentence that consists of fourteen letters. Whenever any of these letters occurs immediately after *al-*, the *lām* is enunciated, meaning it is pronounced clearly and normally. These fourteen letters are known as 'moon letters' because in Arabic one says *al-qamar* (tr. 'the moon'), enunciating the *lām*.

Line 27 is a mnemonic Arabic sentence consisting of fourteen words. The first letter (as opposed to every letter in the mnemonic of line 25) of each word is significant: whenever any of these letters occurs immediately after *al-*, the *lām* is assimilated into the letter after it, meaning that the letter following the *lām* is doubled and the *lām* is not pronounced at all. These fourteen letters are known as 'sun letters' because in Arabic one says *aš-šams* (tr. 'the sun'), assimilating the *lām* into the *šīn* after it. If a *nūn* is the letter after *al-*, nasalization should be extended, as is the case whenever a *nūn* is doubled.

Examples of sun and moon letters are detailed in the chart below:

Moon Letter	**Example**
hamzah	﴿ٱلۡأٓيَٰتِ﴾ *(Al-Baqarah,* 2:118*)*
bā'	﴿ٱلۡبَصِيرُ﴾ *(Al-Isrā',* 17:1*)*

Sun Letter	**Example**
ṭā'	﴿ٱلطَّآمَّةُ﴾ *(An-Nāzi'āt,* 79:34*)*
ṯā'	﴿ٱلثَّوَابِ﴾ *(Āl-'Imrān,* 3:195*)*

Moon Letter	Example
ġayn	﴿ٱلْغَفُورُ﴾ *(Yūnus,* 10:107*)*
ḥā’	﴿ٱلْحَلِيمُ﴾ *(Hūd,* 11:87*)*
jīm	﴿ذُو ٱلْجَلَٰلِ﴾ *(Ar-Raḥmān,* 55:27*)*
kāf	﴿ٱلْكَرِيمِ﴾ *(Al-Mu’minūn,* 23:116*)*
wāw	﴿ٱلْوَدُودُ﴾ *(Al-Burūj,* 85:14*)*
ḵā’	﴿ٱلْخَبِيرُ﴾ *(Al-An‘ām,* 6:18*)*
fā’	﴿ٱلْفَتَّاحُ﴾ *(Saba’,* 34:26*)*
‘ayn	﴿ٱلْعَلِيمُ﴾ *(Al-Baqarah,* 2:32*)*
qāf	﴿ٱلْقَدِيرُ﴾ *(Ar-Rūm,* 30:54*)*
yā’	﴿ٱلْيَوْمَ﴾ *(Al-Baqarah,* 2:249*)*
mīm	﴿ٱلْمَلِكُ﴾ *(Yūsuf,* 12:43*)*
hā’	﴿ٱلْهَدْىِ﴾ *(Al-Baqarah,* 2:196*)*

Sun Letter	Example
ṣād	﴿ٱلصَّٰدِقِينَ﴾ *(Al-Mā’idah,* 5:119*)*
rā’	﴿ٱلرَّٰكِعِينَ﴾ *(Al-Baqarah,* 2:43*)*
tā’	﴿ٱلتَّٰبِعِينَ﴾ *(An-Nūr,* 24:31*)*
ḍād	﴿ٱلضَّآلِّينَ﴾ *(Al-Fātiḥah,* 1:7*)*
ḏāl	﴿وَٱلذَّٰكِرِينَ﴾ *(Al-Aḥzāb,* 33:35*)*
nūn	﴿ٱلنَّاسِ﴾ *(Al-Baqarah,* 2:8*)*
dāl	﴿ٱلدِّينِ﴾ *(Al-Fātiḥah,* 1:4*)*
sīn	﴿ٱلسَّٰٓئِحُونَ﴾ *(At-Tawbah,* 9:112*)*
ẓā’	﴿ٱلظَّٰلِمِينَ﴾ *(Al-Baqarah,* 2:35*)*
zāy	﴿ٱلزُّجَاجَةُ﴾ *(An-Nūr,* 24:35*)*
šīn	﴿ٱلشَّيْطَٰنُ﴾ *(Al-Baqarah,* 2:36*)*
lām	﴿ٱلَّيْلِ﴾ *(Al-Baqarah,* 2:164*)*

The Verbal *Lām*
(Line 29)

29 وَأَظْهِرَنَّ لَامَ فِعْلٍ مُطْلَقَا فِي نَحْوِ قُلْ نَعَمْ وَقُلْنَا وَالْتَقَى

29 Enunciate the verbal lām unconditionally in the likes of 'qul na'am', 'qulnā', and 'iltaqā'.

Unlike the *lām* of the definite article *al-*, the unvowelled verbal *lām* is enunciated, meaning that it is not assimilated into the letter after it, whether the verb is past, present, or imperative. It is also enunciated wherever it appears in the word. The examples provided in line 29 are found in: *Aṣ-Ṣāffāt*, 37:18; *Al-Baqarah*, 2:34; and *Āl-'Imrān*, 3:155.

The exception to this rule is when the unvowelled verbal *lām* occurs in the final position of a word and is followed by another *lām* or *rā'* in a subsequent word. In this case, the unvowelled verbal *lām* is assimilated into the letter after it. I have added the following verses after verse 29 to clarify the exception:

- إِلَّا لِإِدْغَامٍ بِلَامٍ أَوْ بِرَا مَفْصُولَتَيْنِ نَحْوُ قُل رَّبِّ يَرَى
- وَهَكَذَا فِي نَحْوِ قُل لَّنْ يَا فَتَى إِدْغَامُهَا فِي الْحَالَتَيْنِ ثَبَتَا

- *Except due to assimilation into a lām or rā' that are separated [i.e. in another word] like in 'qur rabbi',*

- *And similarly with the likes of 'qul lan', young man! In both cases, assimilation is established.*

The examples in the above lines are from *At-Tawbah*, 9:51 and *Al-Isrā'*, 17:24.

Identical, Nearby, and Alike Letters: Introduction
(Lines 30–34)

(**NB**: Lines 30–34 are fairly abstract. A first-time reader can safely skip them. Of these, line 30 is the one with the most practical applications for a beginning reciter.)

30 إِنْ فِي الصِّفَاتِ وَالْمَخَارِجِ اتَّفَقْ حَرْفَانِ فَالْمِثْلَانِ فِيهِمَا أَحَقْ

31 وَإِنْ يَكُونَا مَخْرَجًا تَقَارَبَا وَفِي الصِّفَاتِ اخْتَلَفَا يُلَقَّبَا

32 مُتَقَارِبَيْنِ أَوْ يَكُونَا اتَّفَقَا فِي مَخْرَجٍ دُونَ الصِّفَاتِ حُقِّقَا

33 بِالْمُتَجَانِسَيْنِ ثُمَّ إِنْ سَكَنْ أَوَّلُ كُلٍّ فَالصَّغِيْرَ سَمِّيَنْ

34 أَوْ حُرِّكَ الْحَرْفَانِ فِي كُلٍّ فَقُلْ كُلٌّ كَبِيرٌ وَافْهَمَنْهُ بِالْمُثُلْ

30 *If two letters agree in attributes and points of articulation, then they are identical.*

31 *But if their points of articulation are close to one another and they differ in attributes, they are known as*

32 *Nearby letters. Or, if they have the same point of articulation but differ in attributes, they are accurately referred to*

33 *As alike letters. Then, if the first of each is unvowelled, name it 'minor'.*

34 *Or, if each letter is vowelled, name them 'major', and understand it through examples!*

This section is concerned with how adjacent letters affect one another. Two factors determine the resulting change: how closely related the adjacent sounds are to each other and the vowelization of the adjacent letters.

Consonant Closeness: Attributes and Points of Articulation

Classical Arabic phonetics emerged out of the need to perfect Arabic pronunciation for tajwīd. In the classical model, the sound of an Arabic consonant depends entirely on two phenomena: its point of articulation (Ar. *makraj*) and its attributes (Ar. *ṣifāt*). Thus, if two consonants agree in both their points of articulation and their attributes, they are identical (Ar. *mitlayn*). If, on the other hand, they have the same point of articulation but differ in terms of attributes, they are alike (Ar. *mutajānisayn*). If their points of articulation are close—whether or not their attributes differ—they are nearby letters (Ar. *mutaqāribayn*). The following chart summarizes these categories:

	Identical Attributes	**Differing Attributes**
Identical Points of Articulation	*Identical Letters* Example: ن – ن	*Alike Letters* Example: ث – ذ
Nearby Points of Articulation	*Nearby Letters* Example: ح – ه	*Nearby Letters* Example: ر – ل

If two letters have distant points of articulation, they can be either distant letters (Ar. *mutabāʿidayn*) or nearby letters, depending on their attributes and the relative distance of their points of articulation.

Types of Letter Adjacency

Whenever two letters are adjacent in Arabic, one or both must normally be vowelled.[5] If both are vowelled, it is known as a major (Ar. *kabīr*) adjacency of letters, because any subsequent change would involve a larger change in pronunciation than if one was unvowelled. If the first is unvowelled and the second vowelled, this is a minor (Ar. *ṣaġīr*) adjacency of letters. (The author does not mention the case where the first is vowelled and the second is unvowelled—absolute (Ar. *muṭlaq*)

5 Adjacent unvowelled letters only occur between words and when pausing at the end of a word, thereby removing its final vowel. In the case of adjacent unvowelled letters between words, a change in pronunciation will occur to remove this phenomenon. Such changes include omitting one or more letters or forcing a vowel upon one of the unvowelled letters.

adjacency—because letters in such an arrangement never affect one another.) The categorization and rulings regarding letter adjacency are identical whether both letters are in the same word or occur across two words.

The six permutations of adjacency and consonant closeness are demonstrated below with examples:

	Identical Letters	**Nearby Letters**	**Alike Letters**
Minor Adjacency	﴿ٱضْرِب بِّعَصَاكَ﴾ *(Al-Baqarah,* 2:60*)*	﴿قَدْ سَمِعَ﴾ *(Al-Mujādilah,* 58:1*)*	﴿ٱرْكَب مَّعَنَا﴾ *(Hūd,* 11:42*)*
Major Adjacency	﴿ٱلرَّحِيمِ مَٰلِكِ﴾ *(Al-Fātiḥah,* 1:3-4*)*	﴿بَعْدِ ذَٰلِكَ﴾ *(Al-Baqarah,* 2:52*)*	﴿وَيُعَذِّبُ مَن﴾ *(Al-Baqarah,* 2:284*)*

The Rulings of the Six Permutations According to *Ḥafṣ*

The canonical recitation of *Ḥafṣ* is by far the most common of all Qur'anic recitations. In this recitation, major adjacency has no effect: each letter is enunciated. As for minor adjacency with nearby and alike letters, they are sometimes assimilated (partially or entirely) into the letter after them and sometimes enunciated. The details are beyond the scope of a beginner's text such as this.

In the case of minor adjacency between identical letters, the first letter is assimilated into the second, which is doubled. (If the identical letters are *mīm* or *nūn*, this doubling entails extending nasalization.) An exception to this rule is when the first letter is a long vowel. This can only happen if the first letter is an unvowelled *wāw* preceded by a *ḍammah* or an unvowelled *yā'* preceded by a *kasrah*. (Since *alif* is never vowelled, minor adjacency cannot exist in relation to it, as that would require a vowelled *alif* after the unvowelled one.) In this case, the long vowel is enunciated, and is not assimilated into the letter after it. Examples of this exception are in the chart below:

Long Vowel	Minor Adjacency of Identical Letters Without Assimilation
wāw	﴿ءَامَنُوا۟ وَمَا﴾ *(Al-Baqarah, 2:9)*
yā'	﴿فِى يَوْمَيْنِ﴾ *(Al-Baqarah, 2:203)*

In addition to this exception, there is one place in the Qur'an where the recitation of *Ḥafṣ* allows for two different readings:

﴿مَآ أَغْنَىٰ عَنِّى مَالِيَهْ ۜ ﴿٢٨﴾ هَلَكَ عَنِّى سُلْطَٰنِيَهْ ﴿٢٩﴾﴾

When reciting verses 28–29 of *Al-Ḥāqqah* (69) together, the reciter may either pause briefly without taking a breath (thereby enunciating the first *hā'*) or assimilate the first into the second, thereby doubling it. The preferred method of recitation is the first.

Long Vowels: Primary Long Vowels
(Lines 35–37)

35 وَالْمَدُّ أَصْلِيٌّ وَفَرْعِيٌّ لَهُ　　وَسَمِّ أَوَّلاً طَبِيعِيًّا وَهُو

36 مَا لاَ تَوَقُّفٌ لَهُ عَلَى سَبَبْ　　وَلاَ بِدُونِهِ الْحُرُوفُ تُجْتَلَبْ

37 بَلْ أَيُّ حَرْفٍ غَيْرِ هَمْزٍ أَوْ سُكُونْ　　جَا بَعْدَ مَدٍّ فَالطَّبِيْعِيَّ يَكُونْ

35 *A long vowel is either primary or secondary. Name the first 'natural', and it is:*

36 *That which does not depend on any cause, nor are letters properly effected without it.*

37 *Rather, if any letter other than a hamzah or an unvowelled [letter] follows a long vowel, it is natural.*

Long vowels are either native to Arabic pronunciation or specific to Qur'anic recitation. The former are primary long vowels, also known as naturally long vowels, because proper Arabic pronunciation cannot be effected without them. A naturally long vowel is with one of the following:

1. An *alif* (which is always unvowelled) preceded by a letter with a *fatḥah*;
2. An unvowelled *wāw* preceded by a letter with a *ḍammah*; or

3. An unvowelled *yāʾ* preceded by a letter with a *kasrah*.

If any of the above is followed by a *hamzah* or unvowelled letter, it is a secondary long vowel whose particular elongation is specific to Qur'anic recitation. If it is not, such that it is followed by a vowelled letter other than a *hamzah*, it is a naturally long vowel. The exception to this rule is the case of long vowels due to substitution (Ar. *madd al-badal*), a type of secondary long vowel where the *hamzah* precedes one of the above. (Substitution vowels are discussed in a later section.)

Vowel Duration

The standard *fatḥah*, *ḍammah*, and *kasrah* are the basic units of time measurement: each takes the time of one count. Naturally long vowels last two counts each.

Long Vowels: Secondary Long Vowels
(Lines 38–40)

38 وَالآخَرُ الْفَرْعِيُّ مَوْقُوفٌ عَلَى   سَبَبْ كَهَمْزٍ أَوْ سُكُونٍ مُسْجَلا

39 حُرُوفُهُ ثَلاثَةٌ فَعِيهَا   مِنْ لَفْظِ وَايٍ وَهْيَ فِي نُوحِيها

40 وَالْكَسْرُ قَبْلَ الْيَا وَقَبْلَ الْوَاوِ ضَمْ   شَرْطٌ وَفَتْحٌ قَبْلَ أَلْفٍ يُلْتَزَمْ

38 *The other, the secondary [long vowel], is dependent upon a cause, such as a hamzah or unvowelled [letter].*

39 *Its letters are three, so make note of them in the utterance 'wāy', and they are found in 'nūḥīhā'.*

40 *A kasrah before yā' and a ḍammah before wāw are conditions, and a fatḥah is incumbent before alif.*

A secondary long vowel is a naturally long vowel that is given a special status in Qur'anic recitation due to an unvowelled letter following it or a *hamzah* preceding or following it. The expression '*wāy*' is a simple mnemonic that combines the three essential long vowels: the *wāw*, *alif*, and *yā'*. All three are found in a single word in the Qur'an: '*nūḥīhā*' (*Hūd*, 11:49).

Diphthongs
(Line 41)

41 وَاللَّيْنُ مِنْهَا الْيَا وَوَاوٌ سَكَنَا   إِنِ انْفِتَاحٌ قَبْلَ كُلٍّ أُعْلِنَا

41 *Diphthongs are composed of an unvowelled yā' or wāw preceded by a fatḥah.*

Arabic diphthongs are the simple combination of a letter with a *fatḥah* on it followed by an unvowelled *wāw* or *yā'*. They are not long vowels in the sense that the pronunciation of the *wāw* or *yā'* is not extended for a double count. Rather, each letter is pronounced as a single count. (There is a case where they are extended in Qur'anic recitation, which is discussed in a later section.) Examples of diphthongs are:

Diphthong	Example
aw	﴿خَوْفٍۭ﴾ *(Qurayš,* 106:4*)*
ay	﴿قُرَيْشٍ﴾ *(Qurayš,* 106:1*)*

The Rulings Related to Secondary Long Vowels
(Lines 42–47)

42 لِلْمَدِّ أَحْكَامٌ ثَلاثَةٌ تَدُومْ — وَهْيَ الْوُجُوبُ وَالْجَوَازُ وَاللُّزُومْ

43 فَوَاجِبٌ إِنْ جَاءَ هَمْزٌ بَعْدَ مَدْ — فِي كِلْمَةٍ وَذَا بِمُتَّصِلْ يُعَدْ

44 وَجَائِزٌ مَدٌّ وَقَصْرٌ إِنْ فُصِلْ — كُلٌّ بِكِلْمَةٍ وَهَذَا الْمُنْفَصِلْ

45 وَمِثْلُ ذَا إِنْ عَرَضَ السُّكُونُ — وَقْفًا كَتَعْلَمُونَ نَسْتَعِينُ

46 أَوْ قُدِّمَ الْهَمْزُ عَلَى الْمَدِّ وَذَا — بَدَلْ كَآمَنُوا وَ إِيمَانًا خُذَا

47 وَلازِمٌ إِنِ السُّكُونُ أُصِّلا — وَصْلًا وَوَقْفًا بَعْدَ مَدٍّ طُوِّلا

42 *Long vowels have three rulings: obligatory, optional, and requisite.*

43 *[It is] obligatory when a hamzah appears after a long vowel in a single word, and this is known as a 'connected vowel'.*

44 *If each [of the hamzah and the long vowel] is in a separate word, then lengthening or shortening it are [both] optional, and this is the 'detached vowel'.*

45 *Similarly, [it is optional] if the lack of a vowel is contingent upon stopping, like in 'ta'lamūna' and 'nasta'īnu',*

46 *Or if the hamzah precedes [the long vowel], for this is a substitution [vowel] as in 'āmanū' and 'īmānan'.*

47 *The requisite [vowel] is duly elongated if an unconditionally unvowelled [letter] follows a long vowel whether continuing or stopping.*

There are three categories of secondary long vowels: obligatory, optional, and requisite. Each category has one or more types of secondary long vowels.

The obligatory category has but one type: the connected vowel (Ar. *al-madd al-muttaṣil*). This occurs when a *hamzah* follows a long vowel in the same word. It is extended whether one stops at the word in question or continues recitation.

The optional category has three types: the detached (Ar. *al-madd al-munfaṣil*), contingent (Ar. *al-madd al-'āriḍ lis-sukūn*), and substitution (Ar. *madd al-badal*) vowels. Such vowels are optional in the sense that not all canonical recitations of the Qur'an prolong them more than naturally long vowels. The reciter is not free to pick and choose as he wills. Rather, he must adhere to the recitation he has received through a qualified teacher.

The detached vowel is when a *hamzah* follows a long vowel in a separate word. If one stops at the word in question (i.e. before the *hamzah*), it returns to being a natural long vowel, as the only reason it was extended in the first place was the *hamzah* after it. When separate words are written as one in Qur'anic orthography, the result is a detached vowel, not an attached one. Examples of this are:

﴿يَـٰٓأَيُّهَا﴾ - ﴿هَـٰٓؤُلَآءِ﴾

The first word (on the right) contains a single secondary long vowel, and it is detached. The second word contains two secondary long vowels: the first is detached and the second is attached. The words *yā* and *hā* are separate words, even though they are orthographically connected to the words after them.

The contingent vowel is when a long vowel or diphthong occurs before a final vowelled consonant whose vowel has been omitted because one has stopped at the word in question. The substitution vowel is when a *hamzah* is followed by a long vowel.

The requisite vowel occurs when a long vowel is followed by a letter that is unconditionally unvowelled, meaning that it is not unvowelled because one has chosen to stop at it, but rather, that its lack of a vowel is intrinsic to the word. This includes when a long vowel is followed by a doubled letter, as a doubled letter is actually two letters: the first being unvowelled and the second vowelled. It also includes many of the letter combinations at the start of many chapters of the Qur'an. There are a total of four subcategories of requisite vowels; further details are present in the following section.

The chart below, and continued on the following page, details the various secondary vowels with examples and their durations according to the canonical recitation of *Ḥafṣ* according to the transmission of *aš-Šāṭibiyyah*:

Secondary Vowel	*alif*	*wāw*	*yā'*	Duration	Effected When Stopping or Continuing
Connected	﴿جَآءَ﴾ *(An-Nisā', 4:43)*	﴿ٱلسُّوٓءَ﴾ *(An-Nisā', 4:17)*	﴿سِيٓءَ﴾ *(Hūd, 11:77)*	4–5 Must be equal to or longer than detached vowel	Both
Detached	﴿بِمَآ أُنزِلَ﴾ *(Al-Baqarah, 2:4)*	﴿قُوٓاْ أَنفُسَكُمْ﴾ *(At-Taḥrīm, 66:6)*	﴿فِيٓ أُمِّهَا﴾ *(Al-Qaṣaṣ, 28:59)*	4–5 Must be equal to or shorter than connected vowel	Only when continuing
Contingent with Long Vowel	﴿ٱلْحِسَابِ﴾ *(Al-Baqarah, 2:202)*	﴿تَعْلَمُونَ﴾ *(Al-Baqarah, 2:22)*	﴿نَسْتَعِينُ﴾ *(Al-Fātiḥah, 1:5)*	2, 4, or 6	Only when stopping

The reciter should be consistent in recitation: if the contingent vowel is prolonged to a count of six once, it should be maintained throughout recitation. The same holds for all other selections. In addition, the duration of the detached vowel must be shorter than or equal to the connected vowel, so reciting

Secondary Vowel	*alif*	*wāw*	*yā'*	Duration	Effected When Stopping or Continuing
Contingent with Diphthong	Impossible	﴿خَوْفٍ﴾ (*Qurayš*, 106:4)	﴿قُرَيْشٍ﴾ (*Qurayš*, 106:1)	2, 4, or 6	Only when stopping
Substitution	﴿ءَامَنُوا﴾ (*Al-Baqarah*, 2:9)	﴿أُوتُوا﴾ (*Al-Baqarah*, 2:101)	﴿إِيمَانًا﴾ (*Āl-ʿImrān*, 3:173)	2	Both
Requisite	﴿الضَّالِّينَ﴾ (*Al-Fātiḥah*, 1:7)	﴿نٓ﴾ (*Al-Qalam*, 68:1)	﴿حمٓ﴾ (*Fuṣṣilat*, 41:1)	6	Both

the former with a count of five and the latter with a count of four is not permissible; all other permutations are allowed.

One might have noticed that many renowned reciters keep the duration of the disconnected vowel at a count of two for the canonical recitation of *Ḥafṣ*. Such reciters are following the transmission of *Aṭ-Ṭayyibah*, which is not normally taught to beginners. Standardized printings of the Qur'an follow the transmission of *aš-Šāṭibiyyah* in their orthography. To recite *Ḥafṣ* properly with a shortened disconnected vowel, one needs to learn the handful of places where *Aṭ-Ṭayyibah* differs from the printed Qur'an. One may not simply choose to shorten the disconnected vowel and neglect the other differences between the two transmissions.

Categories of Requisite Vowels
(Lines 48–57)

48 أَقْسَامُ لازِمٍ لَدَيْهِمْ أَرْبَعَهْ   وَتِلْكَ كِلْمِيٌّ وَحَرْفِيٌّ مَعَهْ

49 كِلاهُمَا مُخَفَّفٌ مُثَقَّلُ   فَهَذِهِ أَرْبَعَةٌ تُفَصَّلُ

50 فَإِنْ بِكِلْمَةٍ سُكُونٌ اجْتَمَعْ   مَعْ حَرْفِ مَدٍّ فَهْوَ كِلْمِيٌّ وَقَعْ

51 أَوْ فِي ثُلاثِيِّ الْحُرُوفِ وُجِدَا   وَالْمَدُّ وَسْطُهُ فَحَرْفِيٌّ بَدَا

52 كِلاهُمَا مُثَقَّلٌ إِنْ أُدْغِمَا   مُخَفَّفٌ كُلٌّ إِذَا لَمْ يُدْغَمَا

53 وَاللَّازِمُ الْحَرْفِيُّ أَوَّلُ السُّوَرْ   وُجُودُهُ وَفِي ثَمَانٍ انْحَصَرْ

54 يَجْمَعُهَا حُرُوفُ كَمْ عَسَلْ نَقَصْ   وَعَيْنُ ذُو وَجْهَيْنِ وَالطُّولُ أَخَصْ

55 وَمَا سِوَى الْحَرْفِ الثُّلاثِي لا أَلِفْ   فَمَدُّهُ مَدًّا طَبِيعِيًّا أُلِفْ

56 وَذَاكَ أَيْضًا فِي فَوَاتِحِ السُّوَرْ   فِي لَفْظِ حَيٌّ طَاهِرٌ قَدِ انْحَصَرْ

57 وَيَجْمَعُ الْفَوَاتِحَ الأَرْبَعْ عَشَرْ   صِلْهُ سُحَيْرًا مَنْ قَطَعْكَ ذَا اشْتَهَرْ

48 *The categories of requisite [vowels] with them [(i.e. scholars)] are four: word-level and letter-level, [combined] with:*

49 *Each appearing as undoubled or doubled; so these are four [categories], to be detailed.*

50 *If an unvowelled [letter] is in the same word as a long vowel, it is word-level,*

51 *But if it [(i.e. an unvowelled letter)] is present in a triliteral letter with a medial long vowel, it is letter-level.*

52 *Each is doubled if assimilated and undoubled if not assimilated.*

53 *The letter-level requisite vowel is at the start of chapters [of the Qur'an], and it is limited to eight letters.*

54 *They are found in the letters of 'How scarce was the honey!' And ʿayn can be recited two ways, but extending [it] is superior.*

55 *Everything other than triliteral letters—other than alif—is known to have a naturally long vowel.*

56 *They are also at the start of chapters and are limited to the expression, 'alive, pure'.*

57 *And the fourteen opening [letters] are found in 'Establish ties during the brief pre-dawn period with the one who cut you off.'*

Requisite vowels are either word-level or letter-level. Furthermore, each of the two types is either doubled or undoubled, for a total of four categories. Letter-level requisite vowels refer to the letter combinations that occur at the beginning of chapters of the Qur'an while word-level requisite vowels are those that appear in complete words.

Word-Level Requisite Vowels

If an undoubled letter that is unconditionally unvowelled (i.e. the lack of a vowel is not because one has stopped at the word, but, rather, is intrinsic to the word) follows a long vowel, this is an undoubled word-level requisite vowel. In the recitation of *Ḥafṣ*, this occurs only in one word that appears twice in the entire Qur'an (*Yūnus*, 10:51/91):

﴿ءَآلْـَٔنَ﴾

If a doubled letter follows a long vowel, it is a doubled word-level requisite vowel. The author refers to doubling as assimilation since the first, unvowelled letter is assimilated into the second. Examples of doubled word-level requisite vowels are below:

alif	*wāw*	*yā'*
﴿ٱلضَّآلِّينَ﴾ *(Al-Fātiḥah, 1:7)*	﴿تَأْمُرُوٓنِّيٓ﴾ *(Az-Zumar, 39:64)*	No such example in the Qur'an

Letter-Level Requisite Vowels

The fourteen Arabic letters found in line 57's mnemonic sentence appear in various combinations at the start of some chapters of the Qur'an. Of these, the eight letters found in line 54's mnemonic sentence all consist of three letters, when spelled out, with the middle letter being a long vowel and the final letter unvowelled. This combination of a long vowel followed by an unvowelled letter makes them requisite vowels. Examples of each are detailed in the chart below:

Letter	Example	Letter	Example
kāf	﴿كهيعص﴾ *(Maryam,* 19:1)	*lām*	﴿الم﴾ *(Al-Baqarah,* 2:1)
mīm	﴿الم﴾ *(Al-Baqarah,* 2:1)	*nūn*	﴿ن﴾ *(Al-Qalam,* 68:1)
'ayn	﴿كهيعص﴾ *(Maryam,* 19:1)	*qāf*	﴿ق﴾ *(Qāf,* 50:1)
sīn	﴿طسم﴾ *(Al-Qaṣaṣ,* 28:1)	*ṣād*	﴿كهيعص﴾ *(Maryam,* 19:1)

The astute reader will notice the middle letter of *'ayn* is not a long vowel, but rather, a diphthong. For this reason, it is permissible to extend this requisite vowel to a count of either four or six, with the latter being superior.

To understand the difference between doubled and undoubled letter-level requisite vowels, it helps to spell them out phonetically. For example, in *alif-lām-mīm*, the last letter of *lām* is assimilated into the first letter of *mīm*, thereby doubling it. Thus, the *lām* is a doubled letter-level requisite vowel while the *mīm* is an undoubled letter-level requisite vowel because the former ends in a doubled consonant while the latter does not. Similarly, in *ṭā-sīn-mīm*, the last letter of *sīn* is assimilated into the *mīm* after it, making the *sīn* a doubled letter-level requisite vowel. Because the assimilation in both cases results in a doubled *mīm*, nasalization must be extended. On a related note, in *kāf-hā-yā-'ayn-ṣād*, the last letter of *'ayn* is pronounced weakly and with extended nasalization according to the normal rules of an unvowelled nūn preceding a *ṣād*.

The remaining six letters found in line 56's mnemonic expression do not have requisite vowels. Rather, other than *alif*—which has no long vowel—they all have naturally long vowels. Examples of each are detailed in the chart on the following page:

Letter	Example	Letter	Example
ḥā	﴿حمٓ﴾ *(Fuṣṣilat,* 41:1*)*	*alif*	﴿الٓمٓ﴾ *(Al-Baqarah,* 2:1*)*
yā	﴿كٓهيعٓصٓ﴾ *(Maryam,* 19:1*)*	*hā*	﴿طه﴾ *(Ṭā-Hā,* 20:1*)*
ṭā	﴿طه﴾ *(Ṭā-Hā,* 20:1*)*	*rā*	﴿الٓر﴾ *(Yūnus,* 10:1*)*

Conclusion of *Tuḥfat al-Aṭfāl*
(Lines 58–61)

58 وَتَمَّ ذَا النَّظْمُ بِحَمْدِ اللَّهِ　　عَلَى تَمَامِهِ بِلاَ تَنَاهِي

59 أَبْيَاتُهُ نَدٌّ بَدَا لِذِي النُّهَى　　تَارِيخُهَا بُشْرَى لِمَنْ يُتْقِنُهَا

60 ثُمَّ الصَّلاَةُ وَالسَّلاَمُ أَبَدَا　　عَلَى خِتَامِ الأَنْبِيَاءِ أَحْمَدَا

61 وَالآلِ وَالصَّحْبِ وَكُلِّ تَابِعِ　　وَكُلِّ قَارِئٍ وَكُلِّ سَامِعِ

58 *This poem is hereby complete with endless praise due to Allah for its completion.*

59 *Its verses are 'incense that has appeared' for those of reason. Its date is 'a glad tiding for whoever masters it'.*

60 *Thereafter, may eternal blessings and peace be upon the conclusion of prophets, Ahmad*

61 *And his people, companions, and every follower, reciter, and listener.*

In accordance with Islamic tradition, the author begins and ends his text by praising Allah and sending blessings and peace upon the Prophet ﷺ. He then broadened his supplication to include everyone who reads and listens; may Allah grant him mercy!

As for his statement that the verses are 'incense that has appeared', it is a symbolic representation of the number 61 using abjad numerals; i.e. the number of the verses in the poem is 61. Similarly, the statement, 'a glad tiding for whoever masters it' indicates that the date of the poem's completion was 1198 AH.

Al-Muqaddimah

Ibn al-Jazarī

Points of Articulation
(Lines 9–19)

9 مَخَارِجُ الحُروفِ سَبْعَةَ عشَرْ عَلَى الَّذِي يَخْتَارُهُ مَنِ اخْتَبَرْ
10 فَأَلِفُ الْجَوْفِ وَأُخْتَاهَا وَهِي حُروفُ مَدٍّ لِلْهَوَاءِ تَنْتَهِي [6]
11 ثُمَّ لِأَقْصَى الْحَلْقِ هَمْزٌ هاءُ ثُمَّ لِوَسْطِهِ فَعَيْنٌ حاءُ [7]
12 أَدْنَاهُ غَيْنٌ خَاؤُهَا والْقَافُ أَقْصَى اللِّسَانِ فَوْقُ ثُمَّ الكافُ
13 أَسْفَلُ والوَسْطُ فجِيمُ الشِّينُ يا والضَّادُ مِنْ حافَتِهِ إذْ وَلِيَا
14 الَاضْرَاسَ مِنْ أيْسَرَ أوْ يُمْنَاهَا واللَّامُ أدْنَاهَا لِمُنْتَهَاهَا
15 والنُّونُ مِنْ طَرَفِهِ تَحْتُ اجْعَلُوا والرَّا يُدَانِيهِ لِظَهْرٍ أَدْخَلُ
16 وَالطَّاءُ والدَّالُ وَتَا مِنْهُ وَمِنْ عُلْيَا الثَّنَايَا والصَّفِيرُ مُسْتَكِنْ
17 مِنْه وَمِنْ فوقِ الثَّنَايَا السُّفْلَى والظَّاءُ والذَّالُ وثَا لِلْعُلْيَا
18 مِنْ طَرَفيْهِما وَمِنْ بَطْنِ الشَّفَهْ فالفَا مَعَ اطرافِ الثَّنَايَا المُشْرِفَهْ
19 لِلشَّفَتَيْنِ الْواوُ بَاءٌ مِيمُ وَغُنَّةٌ مَخْرَجُهَا الْخَيْشُومُ

6 Some editions of this poem start this verse with the following metrically broken hemistich:

لِلْجَوْفِ أَلِفٌ وَأُخْتَاهَا وَهِي

7 Some editions of this poem end this verse with the following metrically broken hemistich:

وَمِنْ وَسَطِهِ فَعَيْنٌ حاءُ

9 *The points of articulation [of letters] are seventeen according to the selection of those who examined [the matter].*

10 *Alif of the cavity and its two sisters are long vowels that stem from airflow.*

11 *Then, from the back of the throat [come] hamzah and hāʾ; then, from the middle of the throat [come] ʿayn and ḥāʾ.*

12 *[From] its [(i.e. the throat's)] very front [come] ġayn and ḵāʾ. The qāf is [from] the back of the tongue [with the palate] above followed by the kāf*

13 *Further forward. [From] its [(i.e. the tongue's)] centre are: jīm, šīn, and yāʾ. Ḍād is from its side when it is adjacent to*

14 *The molars from the left or its right. The lām is [from the side of the tongue that is] closest to its tip.*

15 *Effect nūn further forward from its [(i.e. the tongue's)] tip. Rāʾ is close to this [but] somewhat further back on the base [of the tongue].*

16 *Ṭāʾ, dāl, and tāʾ are from it [(i.e. the tip of the tongue)] and from the upper central incisors. Whistling [letters] are*

17 *From it and from above the lower central incisors. Ẓāʾ, ḏāl, and ṯāʾ are from the upper [central incisors],*

18 *From the tips of both [(i.e. the tip of the tongue and the incisors)]. From the centre of the lip [comes] fāʾ with the edges of the overlooking central incisors.*

19 *From the lips are wāw, bāʾ, and mīm, while nasalization's point of articulation is the nasal cavity.*

The Number of Points of Articulation

During the infancy of Arabic phonetics, there was a difference of opinion regarding how many points of articulation there are in Arabic. After examination, scholars settled on the opinion that there are seventeen points of articulation. This is an approximation, as every letter has its own unique point of articulation.

The First Point of Articulation

The Cavity of the Vocal Tract

There are three long vowels: *alif* preceded by a *fatḥah*, an unvowelled *wāw* preceded by a *ḍammah*, and an unvowelled *yā'* preceded by a *kasrah*. The last two are the 'two sisters' of the *alif*. Their point of articulation is inexact because the vocal tract is not constricted when pronouncing them in the same way it is for consonants. Rather, they are produced by air flowing through the vocal tract.

The Three Points of Articulation of the Throat

The lowest specific point of articulation is for the *hamzah*, at the very back of the throat, followed by the *hā*ʾ, which is slightly higher. Further up, in the middle of the throat, the next point of articulation is that of the *ʿayn* followed by the higher-up *ḥā*ʾ. Two additional letters come from the front of the throat: *ġayn* and *ḵā*ʾ, with the latter having a point of articulation slightly ahead of the former.

The Fifth and Sixth Points of Articulation

The Back of the Tongue

The letter *qāf* is produced by the very back of the tongue hitting the soft palate. Further forward, *kāf* is pronounced by the back of the tongue hitting both the soft and hard palates.

The Seventh Point of Articulation

The Middle of the Tongue

From the centre of the tongue come *jīm*, *šīn*, and the consonantal *yā*ʾ. The Qur'anic *jīm* is similar to the sound pronounced in the word 'jet', and is unlike the French sound found in *jour* despite many Arabs pronouncing it like the latter. The Qur'anic *jīm* is a plosive, or stop consonant, so airflow must cease entirely when properly pronouncing it. This does not happen when pronouncing it like the corresponding letter in French.

The Eighth Point of Articulation
The Side of the Tongue

The letter *ḍād* is specific to the Arabic language, yet many native speakers of Arabic do not pronounce it properly. It is pronounced by pressing the side of the tongue against the insides of the upper molars and pre-molars and gently touching the tip of the tongue at the very front of the hard palate. Either the left or right side of the mouth can be used when pronouncing *ḍād*, with the left side being easier. The tip of the tongue should not be pressed against the palate, as this would result in a stop consonant (which *ḍād* is not) that sounds like an emphatic *dāl*. Another common mistake when pronouncing the *ḍād* is to place the tip of the tongue between the central incisors, which produces a sound similar to the letter *ẓā'*.

The Three Points of Articulation of the Tip of the Tongue with the Hard Palate

The letter *lām* is pronounced by pressing the sides of the tongue closest to its tip along with its tip near the front of the hard palate, behind the roots of the upper central incisors embedded in the gums. When the Divine Name *Allāh* is preceded by a *fatḥah* or a *ḍammah* (or when one begins recitation with it), the *lām* becomes emphatic. This is effected by raising the back of the tongue against the soft palate. When the Divine Name is preceded by a *kasrah*, the *lām* is pronounced normally.

The *nūn* is pronounced with the tip of the tongue touching the hard palate slightly ahead of the point of articulation of the *lām* and is accompanied by airflow from the nasal cavity.

The point of articulation of the letter *rā'* is close to that of the *nūn*, but is slightly further back towards the base of the tongue. Furthermore, when pronouncing *rā'*, a very small gap must remain between the tip of the tongue and the hard palate above it. Pressing the tip of the tongue firmly against the palate forces a trill, causing the *rā'* to roll, which is clearly rejected by all scholars of Qur'anic recitation. On the other hand, leaving too great a gap between the tip of the tongue and the palate results in a sound that is similar to the English *r*.

The Twelfth Point of Articulation
The Tip of the Tongue with the Upper Teeth

The letters *ṭā'*, *dāl*, and *tā'* all emerge from the tip of the tongue touching the base of the upper central incisors. The *ṭā'* is an emphatic *tā'*, pronounced by raising the back of the tongue towards the soft palate. The *tā'* is pronounced somewhat differently than how some speakers pronounce the English *t*. In Arabic, the *tā'* is produced from the base of the upper central incisors whereas some English speakers pronounce the letter *t* from the bottom of the upper central incisors, resulting in a more aspirated sound.

The Thirteenth Point of Articulation
The Tip of the Tongue with the Lower Teeth

The 'whistling letters' (i.e. sibilants) are *ṣād*, *sīn*, and *zāy*. They are produced with the tip of the tongue at the base of the lower central incisors and their sounds emerge from between the top and bottom central incisors. The *ṣād* is an emphatic *sīn*, the difference between the two being that the back of the tongue is raised during the pronunciation of the former. It is a mistake to pucker the lips when pronouncing *ṣād*.

The Fourteenth Point of Articulation
The Tip of the Tongue Between the Teeth

Ẓā', *ḏāl*, and *ṯā'* are produced by placing the tip of the tongue between the top and bottom central incisors. *Ẓā'* is an emphatic *ḏāl*, so the back of the tongue is raised during its pronunciation.

The Fifteenth Point of Articulation
The Lower Lip and Upper Teeth

The letter *fā'* is pronounced by placing the upper central incisors on the inside of the lower lip.

The Sixteenth Point of Articulation
Both Lips

The consonantal *wāw*, *bā'*, and *mīm* are produced from the lips. The consonantal *wāw* is produced by puckering the lips slightly but tightly, leaving a small gap between them. The *mīm* is accompanied by nasalization from the nasal cavity. The lips are pressed more firmly together than in the pronunciation of the English letter *m*.

The Seventeenth Point of Articulation
The Nasal Cavity

Nasalization is produced by air flowing through the nasal cavity. It is an integral component of the letters *mīm* and *nūn*.

May Allah bless Muhammad and grant him peace.

Praise be to Allah, Lord of the Worlds.

Appendices

List of Mnemonics

Line	Mnemonic	Explanation
9	يَرْمُلُون *yarmulūn*	The vowelless *nūn* and *tanwīn* are assimilated into the mnemonic's letters.
10	يَنْمُو *yanmū*	The vowelless *nūn* and *tanwīn* are assimilated with nasalization into the mnemonic's letters.
16	صِفْ ذَا ثَنَا كَمْ جَادَ شَخْصٌ قَدْ سَمَا دُمْ طَيِّبًا زِدْ فِي تُقًى ضَعْ ظَالِمَا *ṣif ḏā ṯanā kam jāda šaḵṣun qad samā dum ṭayyiban zid fī tuqan ḍaʿ ẓālimā*	The vowelless *nūn* and *tanwīn* are pronounced weakly if followed by the first letter of any word of the mnemonic.
25	إِبْغِ حَجَّكَ وَخَفْ عَقِيمَهُ *ibġi ḥajjaka wa ḵaf ʿaqīmahu*	Every letter of the mnemonic is a moon letter.
27	طِبْ ثُمَّ صِلْ رَحْمًا تَفُزْ ضِفْ ذَا نِعَمْ دَعْ سُوءَ ظَنٍّ زُرْ شَرِيفًا لِلْكَرَمْ *ṭib ṯumma ṣil raḥman tafuz ḍif ḏā niʿam daʿ sūʾa ẓannin zur šarīfan lilkaram*	The first letter of each word of the mnemonic is a sun letter.

Line	Mnemonic	Explanation
39	وَاي *wāy*	Each letter of the mnemonic is a long vowel whenever unvowelled and preceded by the appropriate vowel.
54	كَمْ عَسَلْ نَقَصْ *kam 'asal naqaṣ*	Each letter of the mnemonic is a letter-level requisite vowel whenever it is recited by name at the start of a chapter of the Qur'an.
56	حَيٌّ طَاهِرٌ *ḥayyun ṭāhirun*	Each letter of the mnemonic is found in letter combinations at the start of chapters of the Qur'an but is not a letter-level requisite vowel.
57	صِلْهُ سُحَيْرًا مَنْ قَطَعْكَ *ṣilhu suḥayran man qaṭa'ka*	Each letter of the mnemonic is found in letter combinations at the start of chapters of the Qur'an. (This mnemonic combines the previous two.)

Tuḥfat al-Aṭfāl

by

Sheikh Sulaymān al-Jamzūrī

1 يَقُولُ رَاجِي رَحْمَةِ الْغَفُورِ   دَوْمًا سُلَيْمَانُ هُوَ الْجَمْزُورِي

2 الْحَمْدُ لِلَّهِ مُصَلِّيًا عَلَى   مُحَمَّدٍ وَآلِهِ وَمَنْ تَلا

3 وَبَعْدُ هَذَا النَّظْمُ لِلْمُرِيدِ   فِي النُّونِ وَالتَّنْوِينِ وَالْمُدُودِ

4 سَمَّيْتُهُ بِتُحْفَةِ الأَطْفَالِ   عَنْ شَيْخِنَا الْمِيهِيِّ ذِي الْكَمَالِ

5 أَرْجُو بِهِ أَنْ يَنْفَعَ الطُّلَّابَا   وَالأَجْرَ وَالْقَبُولَ وَالثَّوَابَا

6 لِلنُّونِ إِنْ تَسْكُنْ وَلِلتَّنْوِينِ   أَرْبَعُ أَحْكَامٍ فَخُذْ تَبْيِينِي

7 فَالأَوَّلُ الإِظْهَارُ قَبْلَ أَحْرُفِ   لِلْحَلْقِ سِتٍّ رُتِّبَتْ فَلْتَعْرِفِ

8 هَمْزٌ فَهَاءٌ ثُمَّ عَيْنٌ حَاءُ   مُهْمَلَتَانِ ثُمَّ غَيْنٌ خَاءُ

9 وَالثَّانِ إِدْغَامٌ بِسِتَّةٍ أَتَتْ   فِي يَرْمُلُونَ عِنْدَهُمْ قَدْ ثَبَتَتْ

10 لَكِنَّهَا قِسْمَانِ قِسْمٌ يُدْغَمَا   فِيهِ بِغُنَّةٍ بِيَنْمُو عُلِمَا

11 إِلَّا إِذَا كَانَا بِكِلْمَةٍ فَلا   تُدْغِمْ كَدُنْيَا ثُمَّ صِنْوَانٍ تَلا

12 وَالثَّانِ إِدْغَامٌ بِغَيْرِ غُنَّهْ   فِي اللَّامِ وَالرَّا ثُمَّ كَرِّرَنَّهْ

13 وَالثَّالِثُ الإِقْلَابُ عِنْدَ الْبَاءِ   مِيمًا بِغُنَّةٍ مَعَ الإِخْفَاءِ

14 وَالرَّابِعُ الإِخْفَاءُ عِنْدَ الْفَاضِلِ مِنَ الْحُرُوفِ وَاجِبٌ لِلْفَاضِلِ

15 فِي خَمْسَةٍ مِنْ بَعْدِ عَشْرٍ رَمْزُهَا فِي كِلْمِ هَذَا الْبَيْتِ قَدْ ضَمَّنْتُهَا

16 صِفْ ذَا ثَنَا كَمْ جَادَ شَخْصٌ قَدْ سَمَا دُمْ طَيِّبًا زِدْ فِي تُقًى ضَعْ ظَالِمَا

17 وَغُنَّ مِيمًا ثُمَّ نُونًا شُدِّدَا وَسَمِّ كُلًّا حَرْفَ غُنَّةٍ بَدَا

18 وَالْمِيمُ إِنْ تَسْكُنْ تَجِي قَبْلَ الْهِجَا لَا أَلِفٍ لَيِّنَةٍ لِذِي الْحِجَا

19 أَحْكَامُهَا ثَلَاثَةٌ لِمَنْ ضَبَطْ إِخْفَاءٌ ادْغَامٌ وَإِظْهَارٌ فَقَطْ

20 فَالأَوَّلُ الإِخْفَاءُ عِنْدَ الْبَاءِ وَسَمِّهِ الشَّفْوِيَّ لِلْقُرَّاءِ

21 وَالثَّانِ إِدْغَامٌ بِمِثْلِهَا أَتَى وَسَمِّ إِدْغَامًا صَغِيرًا يَا فَتَى

22 وَالثَّالِثُ الإِظْهَارُ فِي الْبَقِيَّةْ مِنْ أَحْرُفٍ وَسَمِّهَا شَفْوِيَّةْ

23 وَاحْذَرْ لَدَى وَاوٍ وَفَا أَنْ تَخْتَفِي لِقُرْبِهَا وَالاتِّحَادِ فَاعْرِفِ

24 لِلَامِ أَلْ حَالَانِ قَبْلَ الأَحْرُفِ أُولَاهُمَا إِظْهَارُهَا فَلْتَعْرِفِ

25 قَبْلَ ارْبَعٍ مَعْ عَشْرَةٍ خُذْ عِلْمَهُ مِنِ ابْغِ حَجَّكَ وَخَفْ عَقِيمَهُ

26 ثَانِيهِمَا إِدْغَامُهَا فِي أَرْبَعِ وَعَشْرَةٍ أَيْضًا وَرَمْزَهَا فَعِ

27 طِبْ ثُمَّ صِلْ رَحْمًا تَفُزْ ضِفْ ذَا نِعَمْ دَعْ سُوءَ ظَنٍّ زُرْ شَرِيفًا لِلْكَرَمْ

28 وَاللَّامُ الاولَى سَمِّهَا قَمْرِيَّةْ وَاللَّامُ الاخْرَى سَمِّهَا شَمْسِيَّةْ

29 وَأَظْهِرَنَّ لَامَ فِعْلٍ مُطْلَقَا فِي نَحْوِ قُلْ نَعَمْ وَقُلْنَا وَالْتَقَى

30 إِنْ فِي الصِّفَاتِ وَالْمَخَارِجِ اتَّفَقْ حَرْفَانِ فَالْمِثْلَانِ فِيهِمَا أَحَقْ

31 وَإِنْ يَكُونَا مَخْرَجًا تَقَارَبَا وَفِي الصِّفَاتِ اخْتَلَفَا يُلَقَّبَا

32 مُتَقَارِبَيْنِ أَوْ يَكُونَا اتَّفَقَا ... فِي مَخْرَجٍ دُونَ الصِّفَاتِ حُقِّقَا
33 بِالْمُتَجَانِسَيْنِ ثُمَّ إِنْ سَكَنْ ... أَوَّلُ كُلٍّ فَالصَّغِيرَ سَمِّيَنْ
34 أَوْ حُرِّكَ الْحَرْفَانِ فِي كُلٍّ فَقُلْ ... كُلٌّ كَبِيرٌ وَافْهَمَنْهُ بِالْمُثُلْ
35 وَالْمَدُّ أَصْلِيٌّ وَفَرْعِيٌّ لَهُ ... وَسَمِّ أَوَّلًا طَبِيعِيًّا وَهُو
36 مَا لا تَوَقُّفٌ لَهُ عَلَى سَبَبْ ... وَلا بِدُونِهِ الْحُرُوفُ تُجْتَلَبْ
37 بَلْ أَيُّ حَرْفٍ غَيْرِ هَمْزٍ أَوْ سُكُونْ ... جَا بَعْدَ مَدٍّ فَالطَّبِيْعِيَّ يَكُونْ
38 وَالآخَرُ الْفَرْعِيُّ مَوْقُوفٌ عَلَى ... سَبَبْ كَهَمْزٍ أَوْ سُكُونٍ مُسْجَلا
39 حُرُوفُهُ ثَلاثَةٌ فَعِيهَا ... مِنْ لَفْظِ وَايٍ وَهْيَ فِي نُوحِيها
40 وَالْكَسْرُ قَبْلَ الْيَا وَقَبْلَ الْوَاوِ ضَمْ ... شَرْطٌ وَفَتْحٌ قَبْلَ أَلْفٍ يُلْتَزَمْ
41 وَاللَّيْنُ مِنْهَا الْيَا وَوَاوٌ سَكَنَا ... إِنِ انْفِتَاحٌ قَبْلَ كُلٍّ أُعْلِنَا
42 لِلْمَدِّ أَحْكَامٌ ثَلاثَةٌ تَدُومْ ... وَهْيَ الْوُجُوبُ وَالْجَوَازُ وَاللُّزُومْ
43 فَوَاجِبٌ إِنْ جَاءَ هَمْزٌ بَعْدَ مَدْ ... فِي كِلْمَةٍ وَذَا بِمُتَّصِلْ يُعَدْ
44 وَجَائِزٌ مَدٌّ وَقَصْرٌ إِنْ فُصِلْ ... كُلٌّ بِكِلْمَةٍ وَهَذَا الْمُنْفَصِلْ
45 وَمِثْلُ ذَا إِنْ عَرَضَ السُّكُونُ ... وَقْفًا كَتَعْلَمُونَ نَسْتَعِينُ
46 أَوْ قُدِّمَ الْهَمْزُ عَلَى الْمَدِّ وَذَا ... بَدَلْ كَآمَنُوا وَ إِيمَانًا خُذَا
47 وَلازِمٌ إِنِ السُّكُونُ أُصِّلا ... وَصْلًا وَوَقْفًا بَعْدَ مَدٍّ طُوِّلا
48 أَقْسَامُ لازِمٍ لَدَيْهِمْ أَرْبَعَهْ ... وَتِلْكَ كِلْمِيٌّ وَحَرْفِيٌّ مَعَهْ
49 كِلاهُمَا مُخَفَّفٌ مُثَقَّلُ ... فَهَذِهِ أَرْبَعَةٌ تُفَصَّلُ

50 فَإِنْ بِكِلْمَةٍ سُكُونٌ اجْتَمَعْ   مَعْ حَرْفِ مَدٍّ فَهْوَ كِلْمِيٌّ وَقَعْ

51 أَوْ فِي ثُلاثِيِّ الْحُرُوفِ وُجِدَا   وَالْمَدُّ وَسْطُهُ فَحَرْفِيٌّ بَدَا

52 كِلاهُمَا مُثَقَّلٌ إِنْ أُدْغِمَا   مُخَفَّفٌ كُلٌّ إِذَا لَمْ يُدْغَمَا

53 وَاللَّازِمُ الْحَرْفِيُّ أَوَّلُ السُّوَرْ   وُجُودُهُ وَفِي ثَمَانٍ انْحَصَرْ

54 يَجْمَعُهَا حُرُوفُ كَمْ عَسَلْ نَقَصْ   وَعَيْنُ ذُو وَجْهَيْنِ وَالطُّولُ أَخَصْ

55 وَمَا سِوَى الْحَرْفِ الثُّلاثِي لا أَلِفْ   فَمَدُّهُ مَدًّا طَبِيعِيًّا أُلِفْ

56 وَذَاكَ أَيْضًا فِي فَوَاتِحِ السُّوَرْ   فِي لَفْظِ حَيٌّ طَاهِرٌ قَدِ انْحَصَرْ

57 وَيَجْمَعُ الْفَوَاتِحَ الأَرْبَعْ عَشَرْ   صِلْهُ سُحَيْرًا مَنْ قَطَعْكَ ذَا اشْتَهَرْ

58 وَتَمَّ ذَا النَّظْمُ بِحَمْدِ اللَّهِ   عَلَى تَمَامِهِ بِلاَ تَنَاهِي

59 أَبْيَاتُهُ نَدٌّ بَدَا لِذِي النُّهَى   تَارِيخُهَا بُشْرَى لِمَنْ يُتْقِنُهَا

60 ثُمَّ الصَّلاةُ وَالسَّلامُ أَبَدَا   عَلَى خِتَامِ الأَنْبِيَاءِ أَحْمَدَا

61 وَالآلِ وَالصَّحْبِ وَكُلِّ تَابِعِ   وَكُلِّ قَارِئٍ وَكُلِّ سَامِعِ

Bibliography

Al-Anṣārī, Z., *Šarḥ al-Muqaddimah al-Jazariyyah fī 'Ilm at-Tajwīd*, 4th ed., Damascus, al-Sham Printing, 1992 CE (1412 AH).

Al-Ḥafyān, A., *al-Wāfī fī Kayfiyyat Tartīl al-Qur'ān al-Karīm*, Beirut, Dar al-Kotob al-Ilmiyah, 2000 CE (1421 AH).

Al-Jamzūrī, S., *Fatḥ al-Aqfāl Šarḥ Tuḥfat al-Aṭfāl fī 'Ilm at-Tajwīd*, Babylon, University of Babylon Press, 2010 CE (1431 AH).

Al-Qārī, M.A., *al-Minaḥ al-Fikriyyah fī Šarḥ al-Muqaddimah al-Jazariyyah*, Damascus, Dar al-Ghawthāni, 2006 CE (1427 AH).

"Makārij al-Ḥurūf al-'Arabiyyah Kulluhā li Faḍīlat aš-Šayk Ayman Rušdī Suwayd", *YouTube*, uploaded by abd Arrachid al djannah, 30 May 2012, www.youtube.com/watch?v=0TSC5XUmIgE

"Tawḍīḥ al-Muqri' Ayman Suwayd li al-Iškāl al-Ḥāṣil bi-Kuṣūṣ al-Ikfā' al-Šafawī", *YouTube*, uploaded by HMA, 28 September 2013, www.youtube.com/watch?v=SUVSi76yvT8

9 789394 834835

Printed at Repro India Ltd.